Contents

Introduction 2

| I | *Alpha Four* (4/4) 4
| II | *Alpha Six* (6/8) 5
| III | *Alpha Three* (3/4) 6
| IV | *Dolphinarts Rondo* (4/4) 7
| V | *Las Vegas Rondo* (4/4) 8
| VI | *Red Hot Rondo* (6/8) 9
| VII | *Dolphin Band is the Greatest Ever* (4/4) 10
| VIII | *Cape Canaveral Rondo* (4/4) 11
| IX | *San Francisco Rondo* (6/8, 3/4) 12
| X | *Palm Valley Rondo* (4/4) 13
| XI | *Syncopation Celebration* (4/4) 14
| XII | *The Mixed-up, Irregular Rondo* (5/8, 6/8, 3/4, 7/8) . . . 16

Body Percussion

SN = Snap   CL = Clap   P = Patsch   ST = Stamp   V = Voice

Memphis Musicraft Publications
4096 Blue Cedar, Lakeland, TN 38002
901-386-8435 • e-mail: MemMus4096@aol.com
ISBN 0-934017-28-X

© 1997 Memphis Musicraft Publications
fourth printing

All rights reserved. No part of this publication may be reproduced or distributed in any form without the expressed permission of the publisher.

The Body Rondo Book
12 Body Percussion Rondos, Elementary to Advanced

RONDO: a musical form based on alternation between a recurrent section and contrasting episodes. The recurrent section must be stated three or more times. There is great variety to be found within the rondo form. ABACA is the simplest. The pieces included in this study are either ABACA or ABACADA. They can be extended by improvising further sections.

The Body Rondo Book is comprised of twelve body percussion rondos for rhythmic study by upper elementary school through adult age students. The first three pieces, the *Alpha Rondos*, are the easiest. They include a lot of repetition, which makes them more quickly accessible to fourth and fifth grade students. The *Alpha Rondos* are also appropriate for a group of teachers to learn in a short time (15 to 30 minutes) at a workshop.

The levels of difficulty proceed, in general, from simple to more complex. There is no age level marking for each piece; some of the more complex pieces have been taught to younger students. Number XI, *Syncopation Celebration*, was taught to a group of sixth graders by a teacher who spread out the teaching over much of the school year and introduced each section with accompanying speech phrases. Numbers VIII, X, XI and XII have been taught to teachers over a period of one week in Orff Schulwerk Training Courses.

TEACHING SUGGESTIONS:

Teach the A section first, and spend enough time on it to ensure proficiency before presenting the B section. Teach the B section and practice ABA. When that is secure enough, teach C and perform ABACA. Apply the same process to the D section if there is one. Depending on the difficulty of the rondo and the ability of the performers, this process may take one practice session or it may be extended over many days (see PACING).

Whenever there are two parts to a section, teach the top part first. When the group has achieved proficiency with that, perform the bottom part while the group performs the top. Then teach the bottom part. When the group has achieved proficiency with that, perform the top part while the group performs the bottom. Divide the group and have them play respective parts.

The instructor should perform the totality of each section before breaking it up into short phrases and echo playing. After the group performs the short phrases well, then echo longer phrases, etc., until they can perform the whole section.

Use a variety of teaching techniques along with rote echo play, i.e., speech phrases, rhythm syllables, scat, notation, locomotor body movement (hear the rhythm while walking the beat, say the rhythm while walking the beat, play the rhythm while walking the beat), etc. Isolate a particularly difficult pattern and work on it at the beginning of each practice session, then perform it within the context of its section. It is especially helpful to have the performers create their own speech patterns for the rhythm patterns or sections that are giving them difficulty.

As cited above, reading notation is only one of the many appropriate techniques for teaching this collection of rondos. Since rhythm reading is an important skill to develop, use of the notation will be valuable as long as it is balanced with other teaching techniques. The use of these other techniques will stretch our abilities on many different levels. Learning by ear (auditory), by feel (tactile) and through movement (kinesthetic) all help to make our musicianship more complete, more grounded in our total beings.

You may wish to teach only the A section of a piece and have your students create the B, C, etc., sections. There are several options here. The new sections can be planned and written out or, after a bit of practice, they can be improvised by individuals or small groups on the spot. It is important to practice improvisation in advance so that students may get ideas regarding the feel, the sound, the length of time they have to improvise, etc. Another option is to have question/answer led by the teacher or a capable student in the new sections. An example of a student-planned section can be found in the C section of number VII. It is comprised of ostinato patterns that the students created. We layered the patterns in and extended the length of that section. The performers benefit greatly from having the opportunity to participate in this creative process because it is an extended application of their musicianship, and the music will then become their own.

Present each section at the correct tempo. This will build in a feel for the proper tempo of the piece. Difficult parts can then be slowed down and practiced before bringing them back to tempo at the end of each practice session.

Use good clapping technique. Hold one hand relatively steady. Avoid excessive motion and constant loud clapping.

Add vocal sounds, dramatic motions, locomotor body movement, unpitched percussion, etc., for special effects if you or the group feel the inspiration. Group involvement on this level also helps to make the music "belong" to the group that is performing it.

Some "helpful hints" pertaining to certain sections will be found following many of the rondos. The section(s) under scrutiny is (are) specified, then ideas suggested.

PACING:

With adults, you might wish to learn one section per day of the more advanced pieces, numbers VIII–XII. After reviewing the known section(s) and learning the new section, always practice them with the correct form, alternating A with the contrasting sections, before the end of the practice session. Practice sessions should be 15 to 30 minutes in length.

In most cases, junior high and high school students can learn by rote one section per day of numbers I–VII. This process greatly helps their rhythmic memory. Reading will speed up the process.

The rate of learning is, of course, slower with elementary school children, whom you may see only once or twice a week, than it is with adults, so be sure to make the A section thoroughly ingrained before proceeding to the other sections. If you are practicing a more difficult piece, spend a few minutes a day over a longer period of time.

Strive to make every practice and performance a musical experience.

—*Jim Solomon*

I. Alpha Four

Jim Solomon

Form: ABACA

A section: Perform for students, then teach the rhythm of the A section with patschen only. Patsch the rhythm again and add the three claps at the end. Add and practice the claps on beat two. Then perform again and ask students to find which measure of the first three measures does not have a clap on beat four. After the students identify the third measure, practice the A section as it is written.

II. Alpha Six

Jim Solomon

Form: ABACA

III. Alpha Three

Jim Solomon

Form: ABACA

A section: Establish the meter and tempo by moving in threes before beginning the A section. Have students take a step on beat one of each measure of the music that you play for them. Then practice the ♩ ♩ ♩ (clap patsch patsch) pattern. Perform the A section and have students identify how many times that pattern occurs. Ask them to perform only that pattern with you the four times it occurs. After they can do this, they can easily add the rest.

IV. Dolphinarts Rondo

Jim Solomon

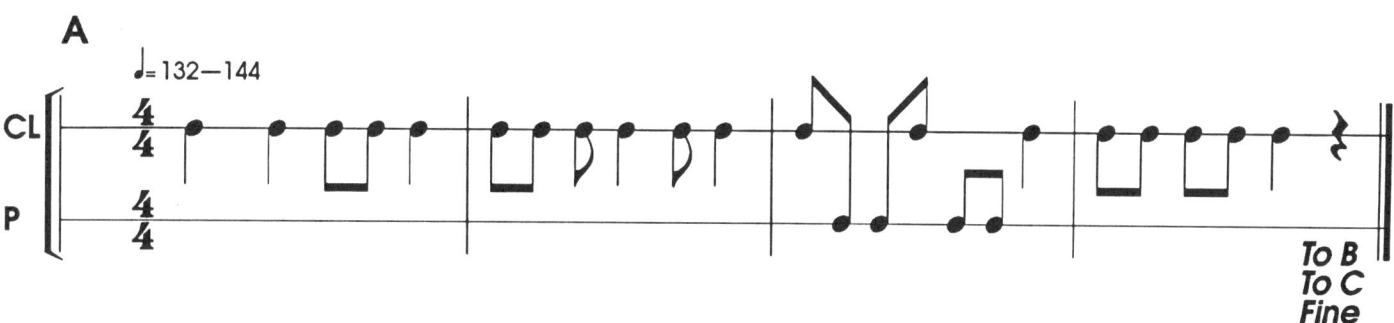

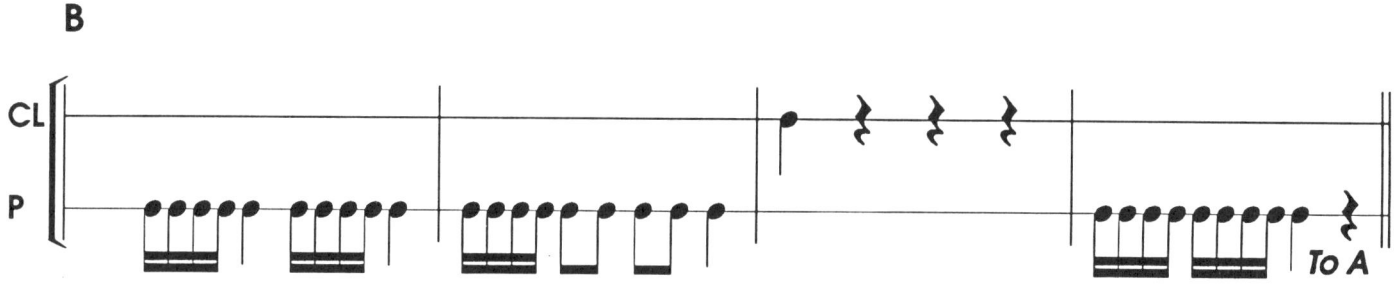

C Walk forward and back or in a circle.

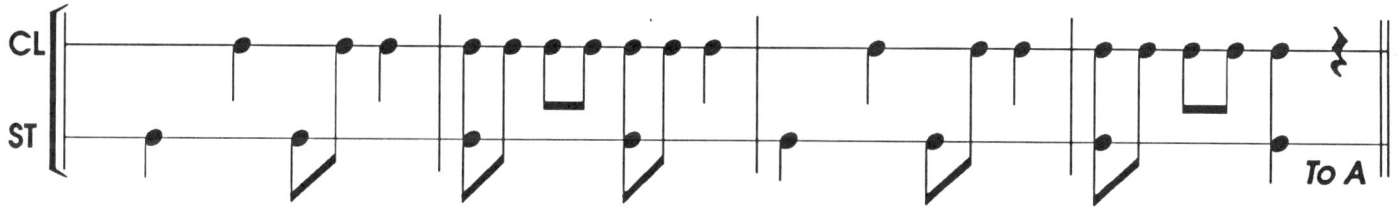

Form: ABACA

A section: Practice the pattern in measure three. Perform A section for students and have them identify where it occurs. Then proceed to learn the whole A section from the beginning.

C section: Perform for students, then have them walk ♩ 𝄾 ♩ 𝄾 , etc., while you echo speak the rhythm. Add the rest of the body percussion measure by measure.

V. Las Vegas Rondo

Jim Solomon

Because body percussion cannot sustain the value of ♩'s, ♩.'s, and 𝅝's, it is necessary to add vocal sound effects to sustain these note values in the A section. Students can use train sounds, whistles, etc., or they can create their own sounds. Emphasize (practice!) keeping the tempo steady.

Form: ABACA

C section: Students should be able to speak the words below the first two measures before they clap them.

VI. Red Hot Rondo

Jim Solomon

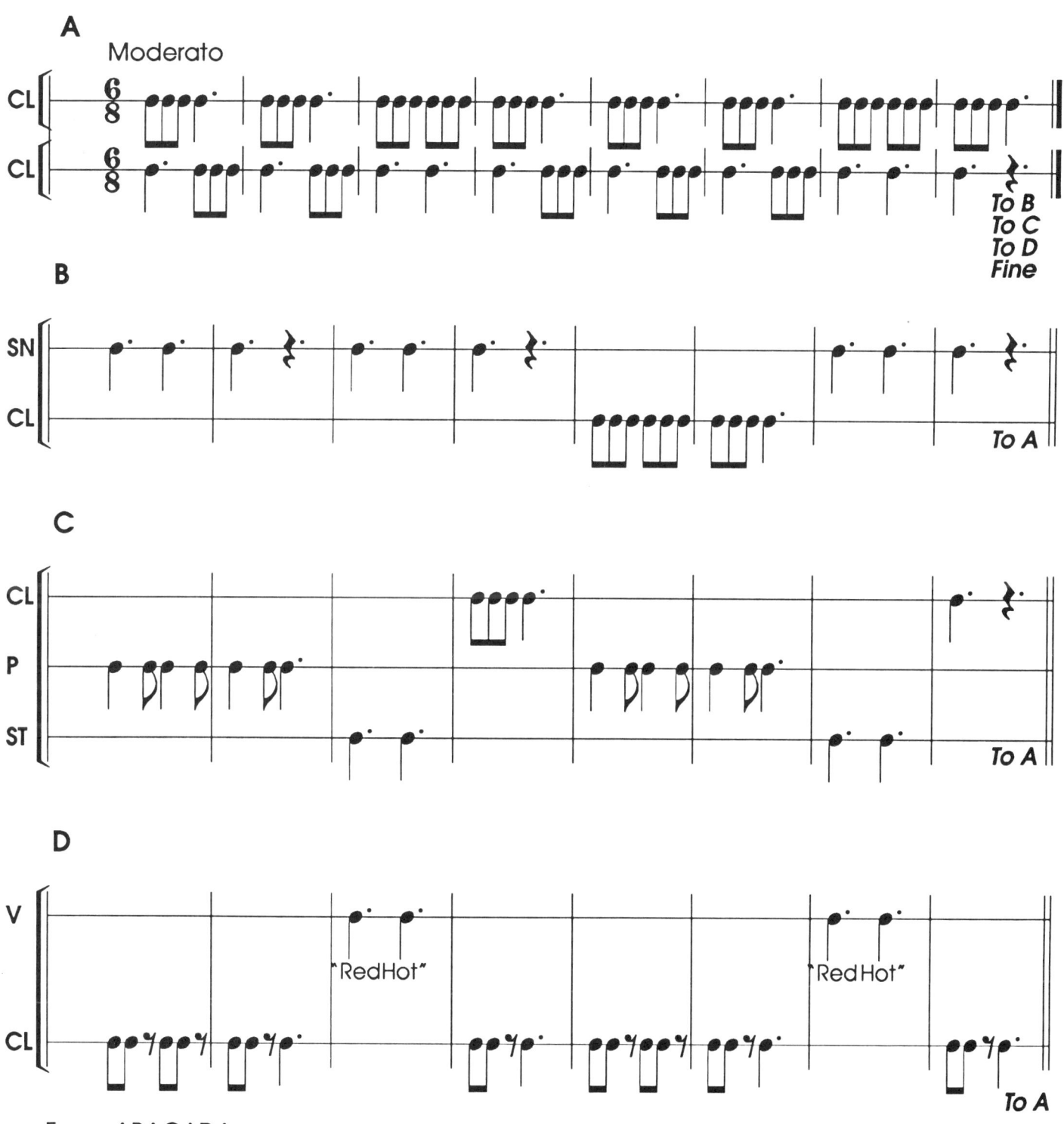

Form: ABACADA

VII. Dolphin Band is The Greatest Ever

Jim Solomon

The title of this piece was created by a student who made up the words to help the group remember the rhythm of the first three measures of the A section. The group created its own C section by creating different rhythm patterns and then layering them in as ostinato patterns one at a time. Your group could do the same thing, or one or more students could improvise the C section.

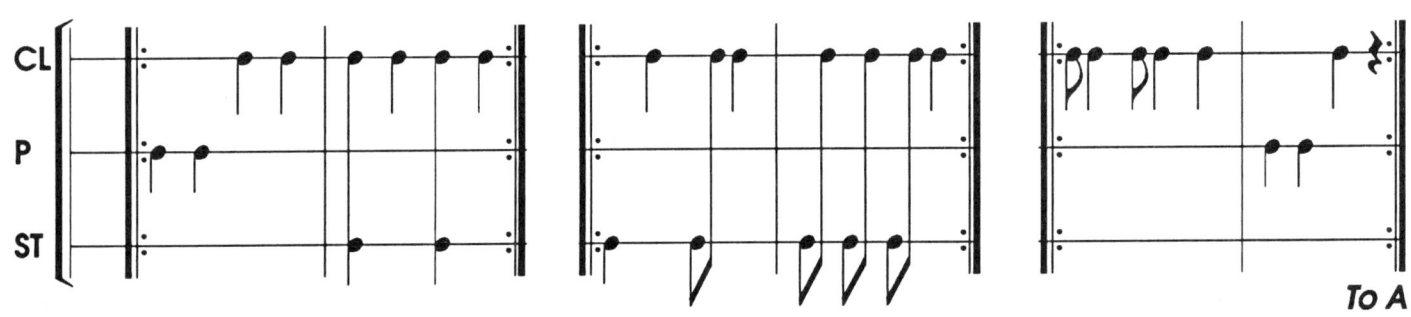

Form: ABACA

VIII. Cape Canaveral Rondo

Jim Solomon

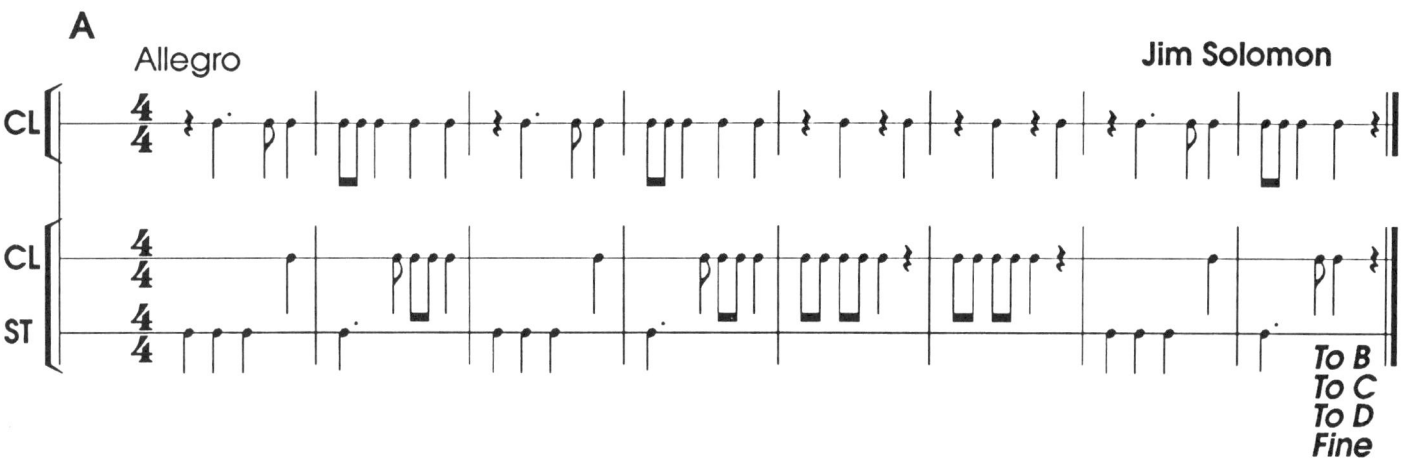

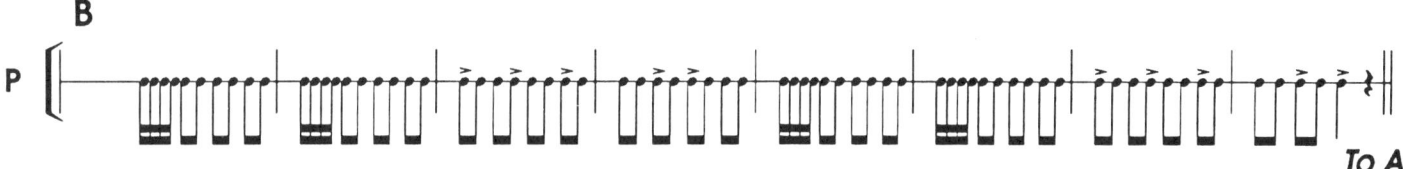

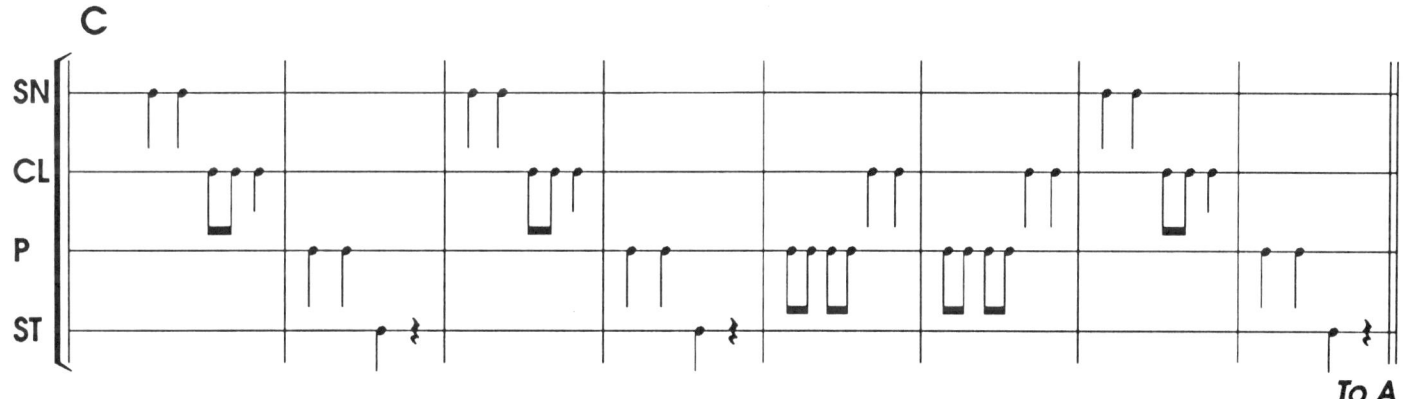

D Have group decide on a walking pattern for this section.

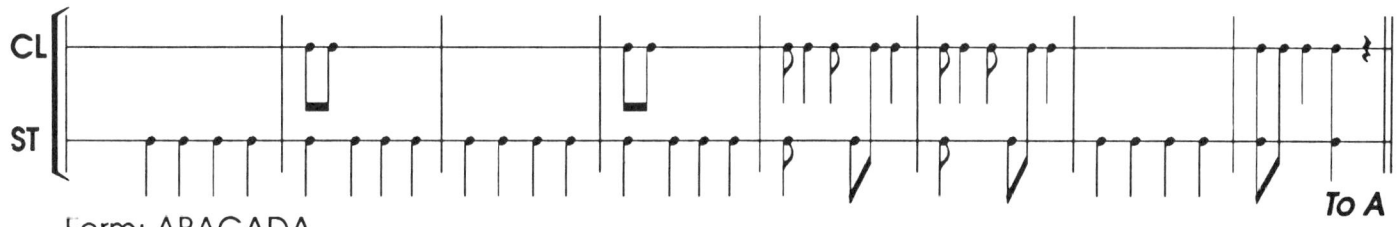

Form: ABACADA

A section: Emphasize to the group with the top clapping part that the rest is **beat one.**

B section: Measures 3 and 4, 7 and 8 have the same accents as the Cuban clave pattern: ♩. ♩. ♩ | 𝄽 ♩ ♩ 𝄽 ; echo clap this rhythm; patsch steady eighth notes and speak the accents; then patsch the eighth notes and include the accents. If the performers alternate their hands while playing this part, all of the accents except the second will be with the hand that starts the pattern.

11

IX. San Francisco Rondo

Jim Solomon

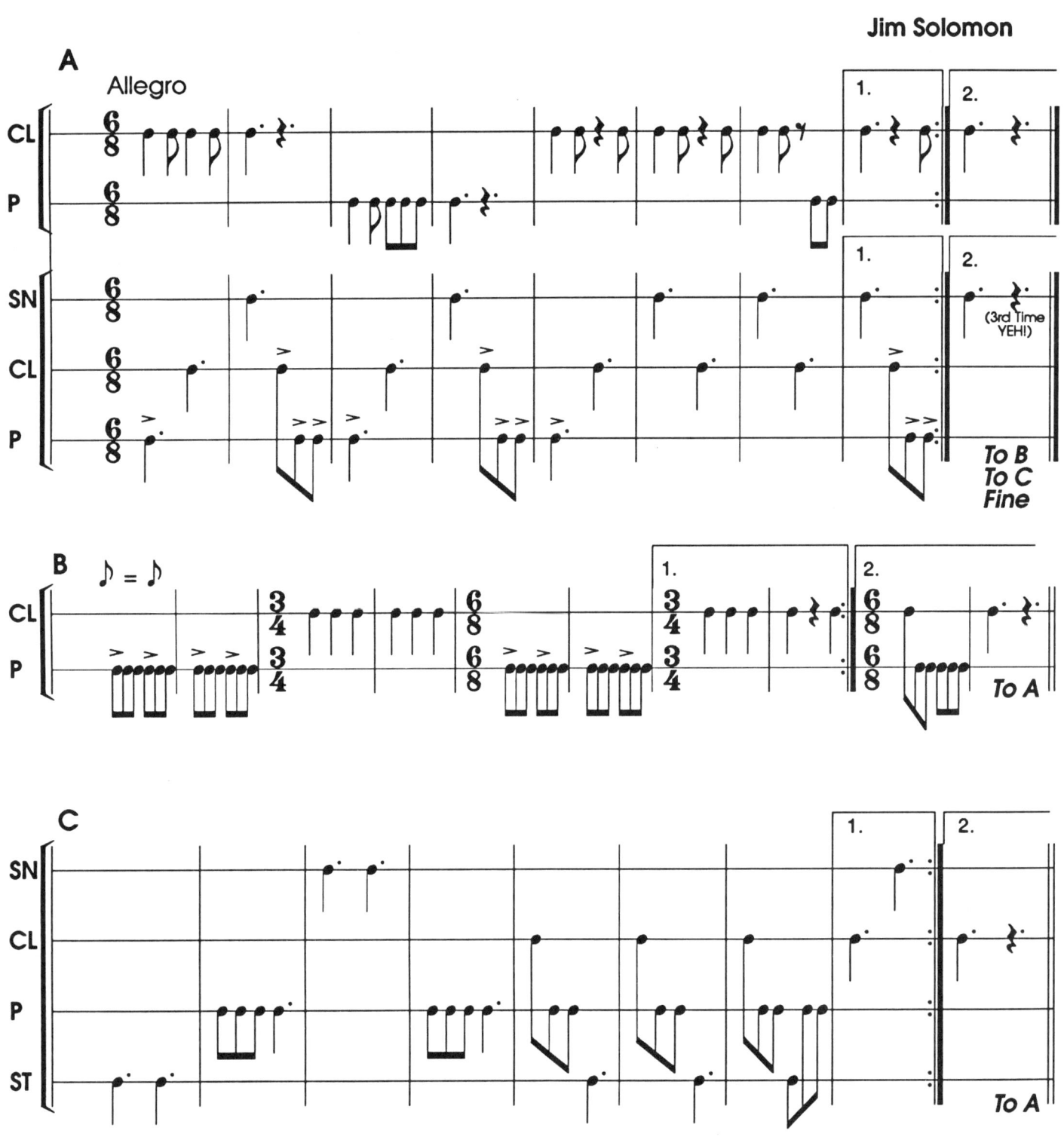

Form: ABACA

C section: Isolate and practice measures 7 and 8.

X. Palm Valley Rondo

Jim Solomon

Form: ABACADA

B section: Note the addition of one eighth note from measure 1 to 2 to 3 to 4. This repeats identically in measures 5, 6, 7, and 8.

D section: Note how the bottom part often reinforces the ♩♫ figure and the claps in the top part.

XI. Syncopation Celebration

Jim Solomon

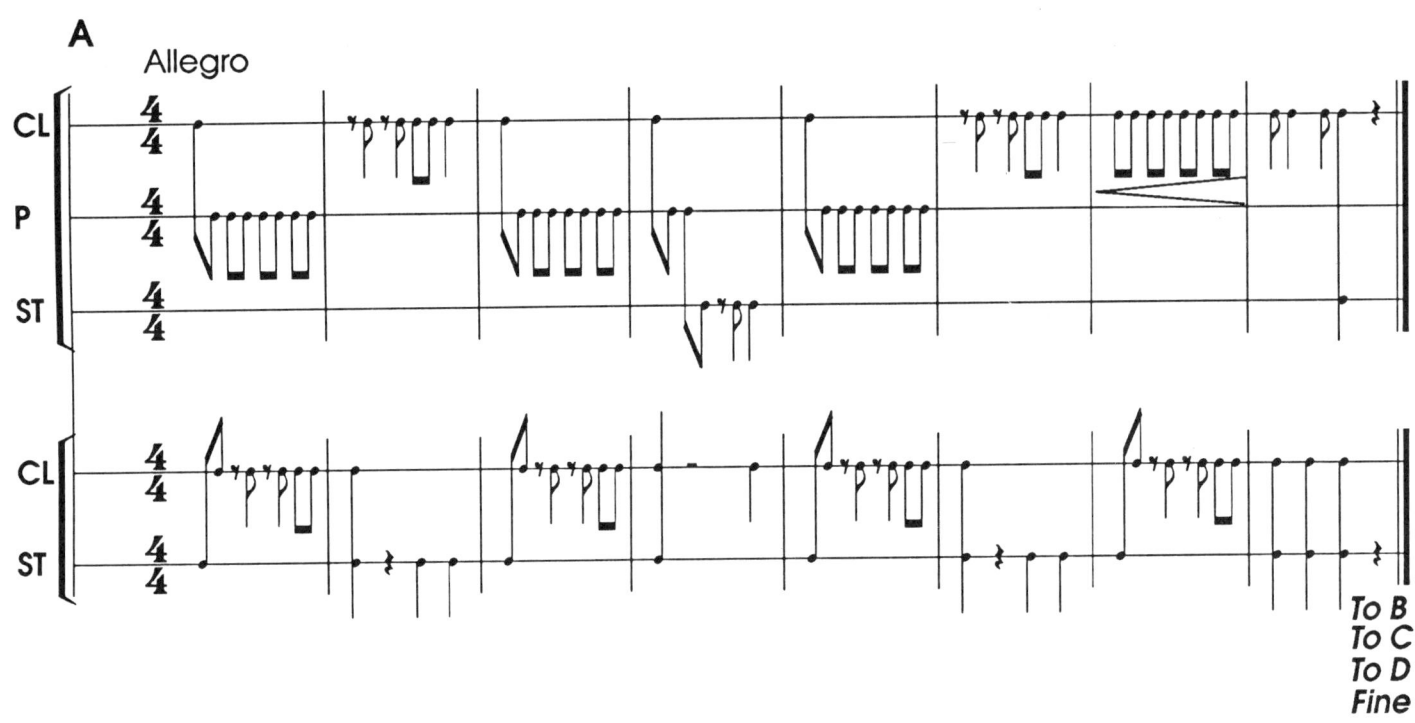

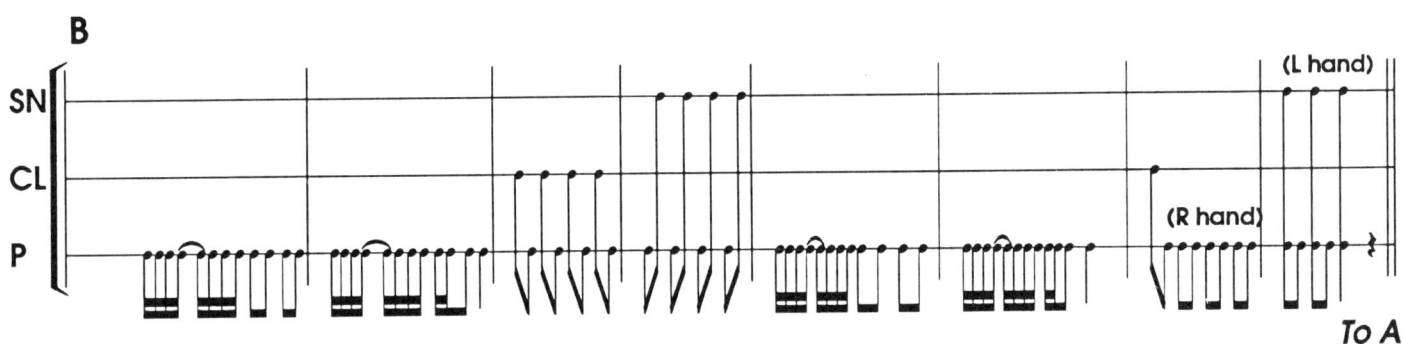

C   Walk in formation or in "chaotic random order."

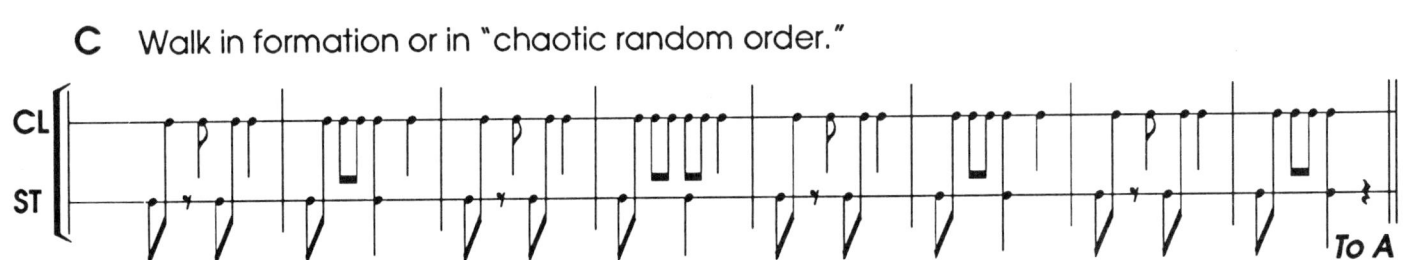

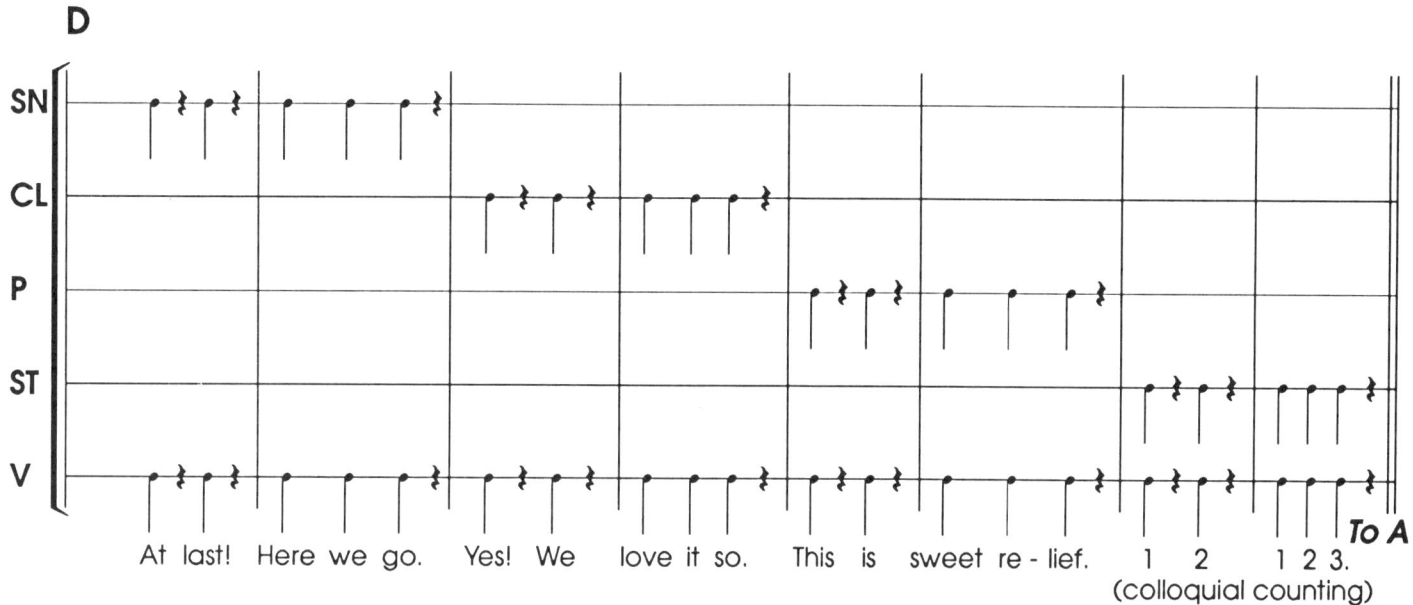

Form: ABACADA

A section: Top Part: When teaching measures 1 and 2, make a strong vocal sound on the first beat of measure 2 so that everyone will learn to feel that rest. Isolate and practice measure 4 every day.

Bottom Part: Isolate measure 1 and the first beat of measure 2 (this pattern repeats four times). Have the group perform that four times while you perform the rest of the body percussion (the "solder" or "glue" between the repetitions of the pattern). Then they can join you.

B section: Note the shift in the patschen part from offbeat to on beat between measures 3 and 4.

C section: Have the group count how many times measure 1 repeats (four). Group performs that rhythm on all odd numbered measures, you perform even numbered measures. Then echo two measures, etc., at a time.

D section: Start speaking with high voices. Lower speaking pitch every phrase (every 2 measures).

XII. The Mixed Up, Irregular Rondo

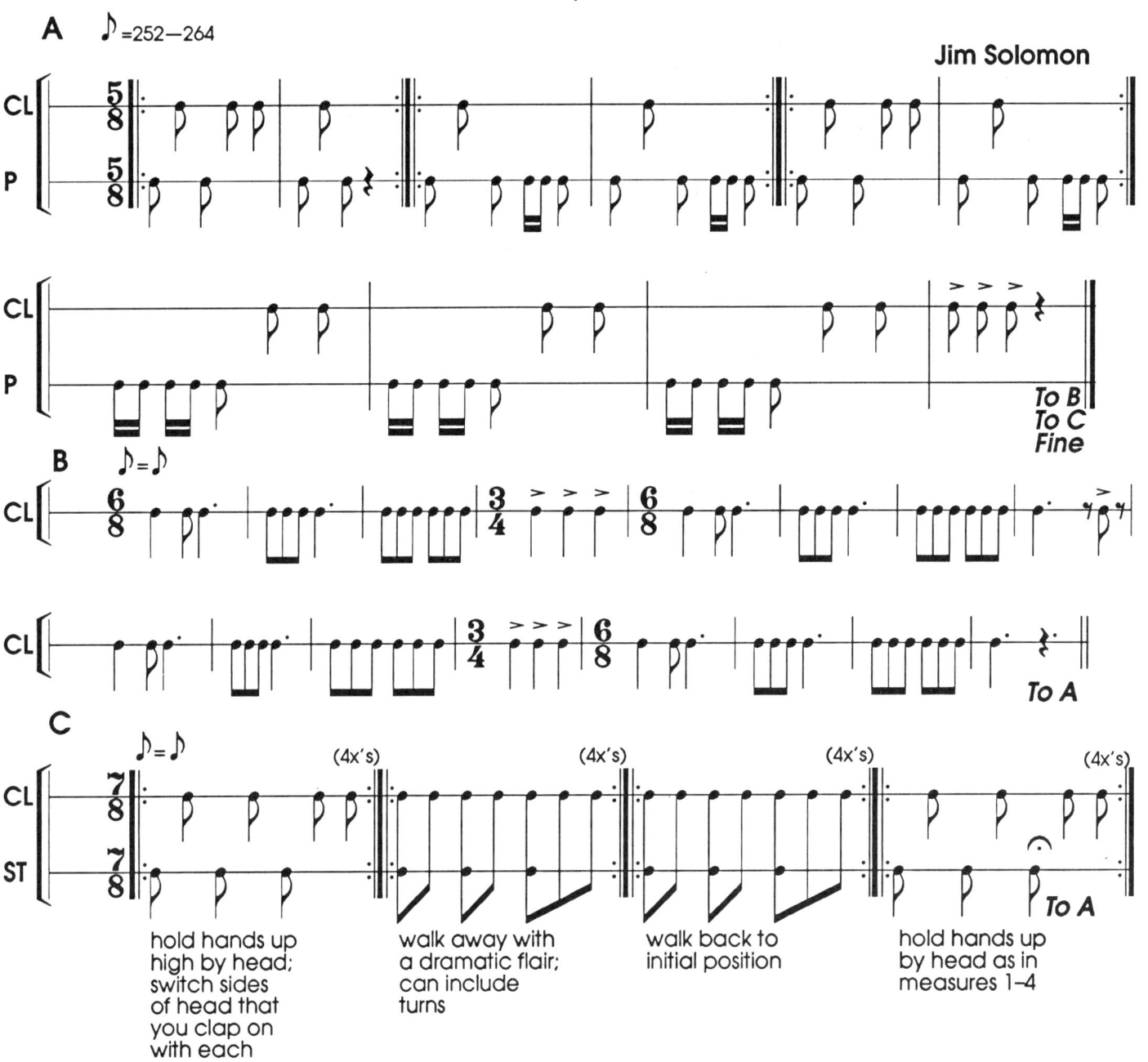

Form: ABACA

Keep the eighth note pulse internally ticking throughout!

A section: Feel the five as two plus three. Move around the room in two plus three (take steps on the accented beats, 1̂ 2 1̂ 2 3, etc.) to get the feel before echoing any patterns. Alternate hands when patsching the sixteenth notes. Use only one hand (i.e., R hand) for the patschen in parts where there are no sixteenths. Keep L hand above leg ready for the claps.

C section: Feel the seven as two plus two plus three. Move around the room in this manner before beginning the body percussion.